AF406278

DEDICATION

Dedicated to my first nephew, Stetson. May your future be full of big, beautiful dreams!

In Texas,
when the sun goes
down, the night is
magical and majestic!

Can you feel it?

The wind rustling in the trees. There is a big breeze!

Here, the bluebonnets grow,

armadillos roll,

and our rivers hum a
soothing flow.

as we roast
hot dogs and
marshmallows.

Hang out and believe,

With your eyes, you will see...

How the fireflies
bounce into stars...

on tunes of an
old guitar.

Climb up the ladder.
Let's lay here and
chatter,

counting each
shooting star.

our dreams will be
deep, of this beautiful
countryside.

GOOD
NIGHT

OTHER BOOKS:
By Aunt Shelly

ABOUT THE AUTHOR

Michelle Kolodziejczyk, pen name *Aunt Shelly,* is a special education teacher in Texas. She loves to help children learn through play, creativity, and imagination!

Scan for more books.

www.shellycreatesit.com

Leave a review!

https://maps.app.goo.gl/TKUad3ZpTPiDeWuw8